AF372181

This book
belongs to:

____

____

____

____

Copyright© 2023. All rights reserved.

First published 2023 with an exclusive licence from the authors to CHEETAH® Purrrrrrr Publishing, an imprint of CHEETAH® Toys & More, LLC (CHEETAH®).

Contact us: 1-860-781-1276, 1-876-909-6311 (WhatsApp),
info@mycheetahacademy.com; paulettetrowers@yahoo.com

ISBN-13: 979-8-3303-4938-8
ISBN-10: 8-3303-4938-8

Dear CHEETAH® family:

Our little books were specially created to help our early readers master their decoding skills and build reading fluency. The repetitive use of high-frequency words, word families, decodable words, rhymes, and vivid illustrations facilitates this process. Our stories complement the objectives and content highlighted in the Jamaica Early Childhood Curriculum Guide and the Ministry of Education and Youth Grade 1 National Standards Curriculum.

In journeying through our series, our little ones will develop a deeper awareness of and appreciation for our Jamaican culture. Our books also have universal appeal, as any early reader can identify with the characters, events and subjects in our texts. Readers will get to enjoy the stories, build vocabulary, and exercise critical thinking by engaging in the activities at the end of each story.

Additionally, as a precursor to our series, or as a support to it, we've created a decodable 'sentence strip' book for the very young readers and those who require more scaffolding.

Happy reading!

CHEETAH®
Chasing and capturing your dreams with you.

C-DER™
CHEETAH Decodable & Early Readers

Never stop learning. The world is your classroom. Let's stay curious!

My decodable words:

call, can, man, today, way,
let, Rick, stick, fun, sun

Letter sound:

- consonant sound /r/ in the initial and final positions in words

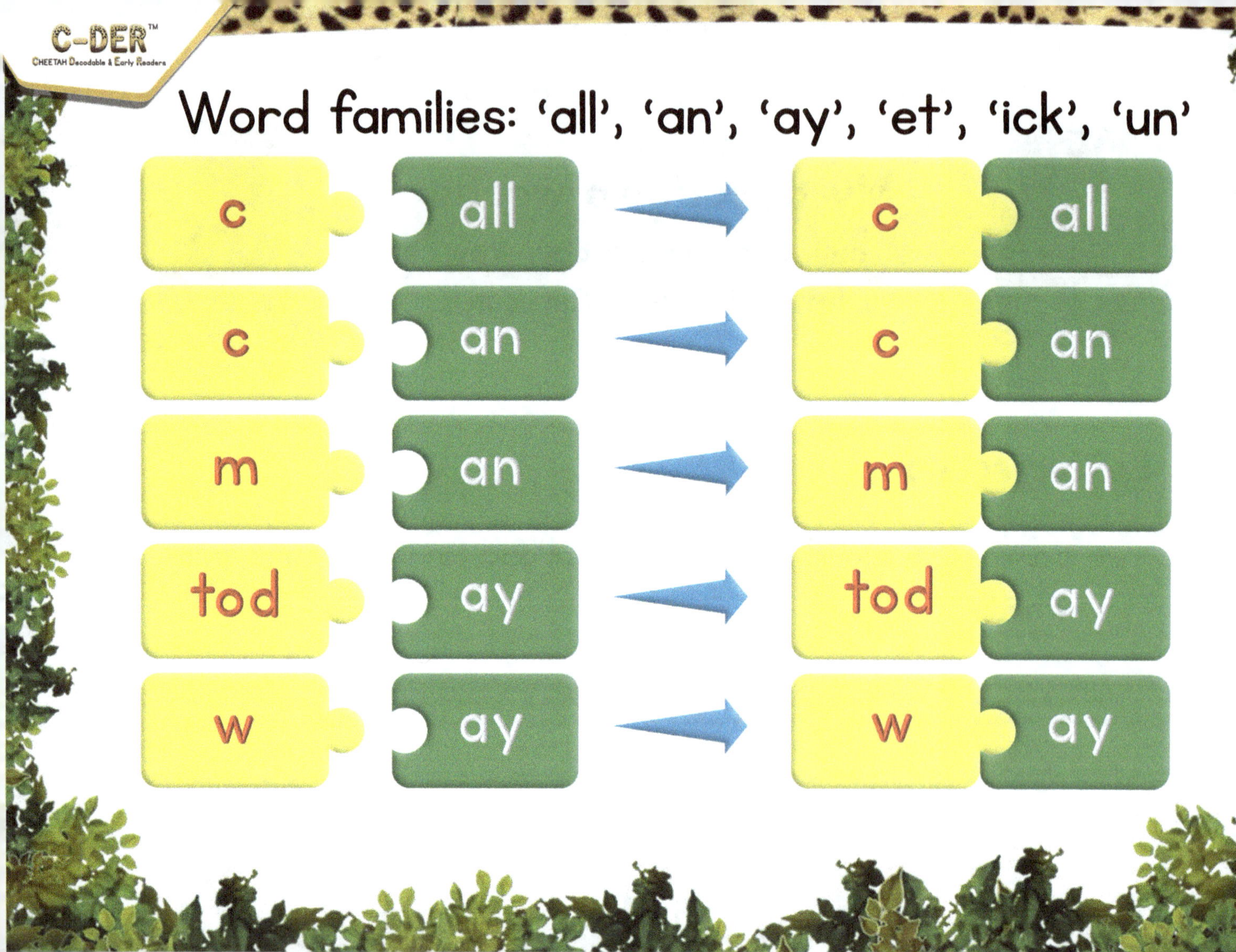
Word families: 'all', 'an', 'ay', 'et', 'ick', 'un'
c all → c all
c an → c an
m an → m an
tod ay → tod ay
w ay → w ay

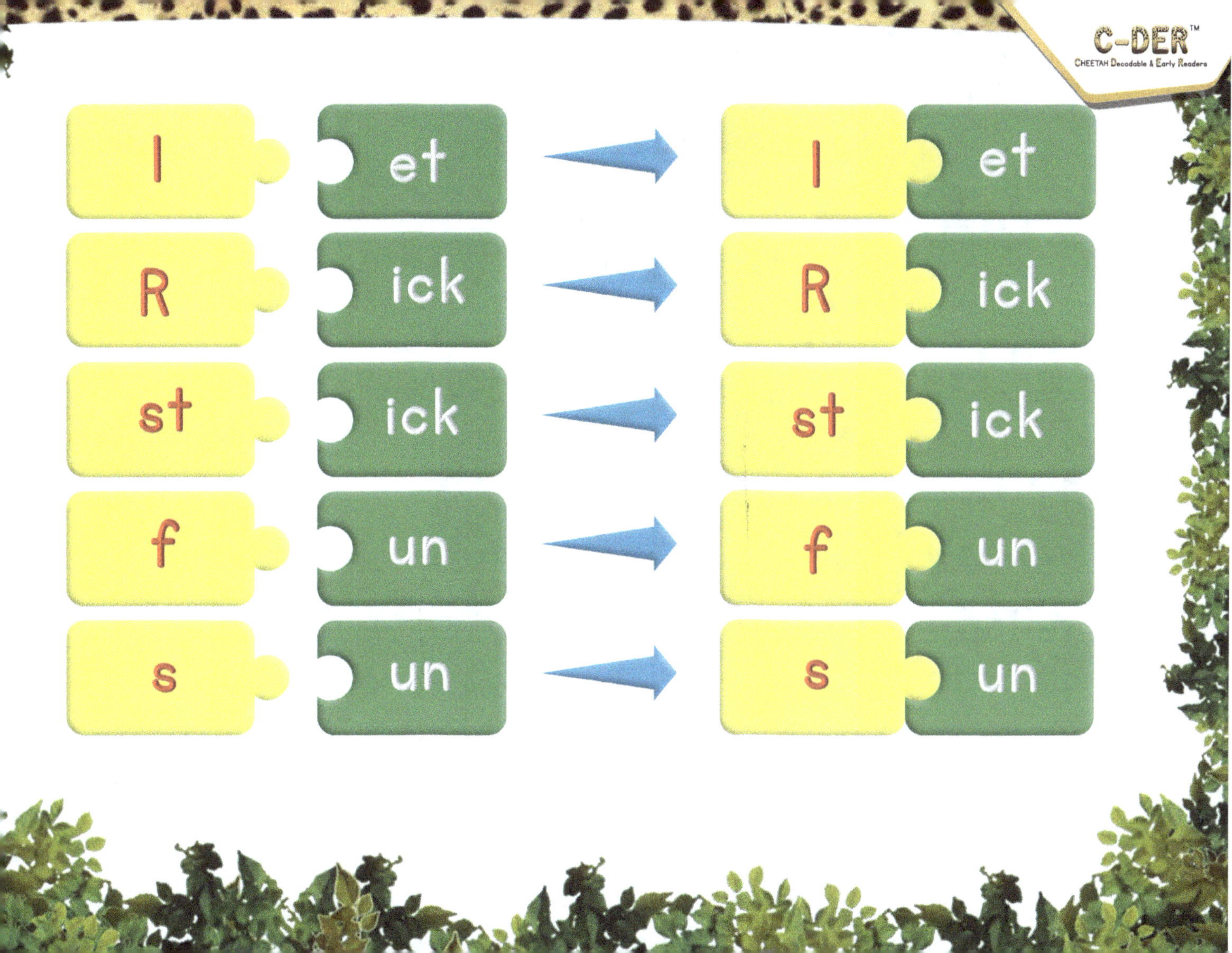

C-DER
CHEETAH Decodable & Early Readers
l et
R ick
st ick
f un
s un
l et
R ick
st ick
f un
s un

C-DER™
CHEETAH Decodable & Early Readers
1

The River Ride

It is a sunny Saturday afternoon.

Mom says, 'We will be there soon.'

They will take a ride on the river today.

They are happy to be on their way.

C-DER
CHEETAH Decodable & Early Readers
3

'We are here!' Rose says with glee.
'Look at the water, Ron. See!
Look at that man on a river raft.
I want to ride on that river craft!'

C-DER™
CHEETAH Decodable & Early Readers
5

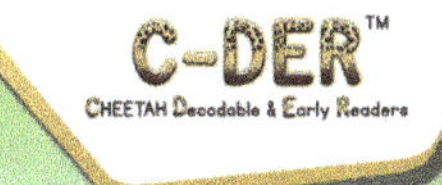

There are other rafts on the water.

They are lined up close to each other.

There are men standing close to the rafts.

They are the owners of the crafts.

Dad goes to talk to a man named Rick.

He has what looks like a very long stick.

Ron asks, 'What does he use the stick for?'

Mom says, 'To move the raft.
It is called an oar.'

Dad calls to them, 'Come now.
Let us go.'

They go down where the rafts
are lined up in a row.

Rick says, 'Two can go on
a raft at one time.'

Rick holds the raft
so Dad and Ron can climb.

C-DER™
CHEETAH Decodable & Early Readers
11

Mom and Rose go on another raft.

Rex, Rick's brother, owns that craft.

Off they go riding down the river.

'Look, Mom,' says Rose, 'a fish! It is silver.'

C-DER
CHEETAH Decodable & Early Readers
13

They can hear the birds sing in the trees.

They enjoy the warm sun and the breeze.

They make a few stops to look at the plants.

They see river crabs, lizards and ants.

C-DER
CHEETAH Decodable & Early Readers
15

They stop to have a drink of coconut water.

'Thank you,' they say to Rick and his brother.

They go back down the river. The ride is done.

Ron says, 'Can we go again soon?
It was lots of fun.'

Discussion and activities:

1. Have the children share their river experiences.

2. Have the children identify the words with the target letter and sound.

3. Have the children make the sound of the target letter and identify rhyming words in the text.

Discussion and activities:

4. Discuss the words *raft*, *craft* and *oar* as used in the context of the story.

5. Have the children read the text aloud.

Learning letters is like collecting colorful feathers for the wings of your imagination.

Questions:

1. What are the names of some of the rivers in your country?

....

2. Why do you think the raft owners were allowing only two people on a raft at a time?

....

www.ingramcontent.com/pod-product-compliance
Lightning Source LLC
Chambersburg PA
CBHW081305130726
47998CB00010B/2939